ST. CHARLES SCHOOL
3250 18TH STREET
SAN FRANCISCO, CA 94110

100 Unforgettable Moments in
The Summer Olympics

Bob Italia

ABDO & Daughters
Publishing

Published by Abdo & Daughters, 4940 Viking Drive, Suite 622, Edina, Minnesota 55435.

Printed in the United States.

Cover Photo credits: Allsport
Interior Photo credits: Wide World Photo

Edited by Paul Joseph

Library of Congress Cataloging-in-Publication Data

Italia, Bob, 1955-
   100 unforgettable moments in the Summer Olympics / Bob Italia.
      p. cm. — (100 unforgettable moments in sports)
Includes index.
Summary: Relates notable events in the history of the Summer Olympics.
   ISBN 1-56239-695-l
   l. Olympics—History—Juvenile literature.   [l. Olympics--History.] I. Title. II. Series: Italia, Bob, 1955-   100 unforgettable moments in sports.
GV721.5.I83 1996
796.48—dc20   96-7597
                                                              CIP
                                                              AC

Contents

The Most Unforgettable Moment?

The Summer Olympics have had many unforgettable moments in their long history. Some of the world's greatest athletes have performed incredible feats and set amazing records. Who could forget swimmer Mark Spitz's seven-gold-medal performance in 1972, or gymnast Nadia Comaneci's perfect "10" in 1976 ?

Some unforgettable moments had nothing to do with world records or superhuman feats. Runner Derek Redmond didn't win any medals, yet he became famous for his competitive spirit.

There is no one most unforgettable moment in Olympic history. The following events are in chronological order, not ranked according to importance. That judgment remains in the hearts of sports fans who have made this worldwide event so special.

Opposite page: Wilma Rudolph gets off to a flying start in the 200-meter sprint.

The "First" Olympics

Because of the city's historical ties to the ancient Olympics, Athens, Greece, was the only logical choice as host of the Olympic Games when they were revived in 1896.

The first Olympics did not resemble today's highly-publicized and well-organized event. There were no national committees or formally trained teams. Fourteen countries and 245 athletes entered the Games. Many of the competitors paid their own way.

Not surprising, Greece had the most athletes. The host country had its national pride at stake, and looked to perform well. But much to their dismay, American athletes won 9 of the 11 track and field events. Australia won the other two. The Greek athletes could not win a single event.

On the final day of the track and field competition, the marathon run was scheduled. Losing this race would be the ultimate Greek tragedy, for the event was born from the Battle of Marathon in 490 B.C., when Greek warriors defeated invading Persians on the Plains of Marathon, a sea town 25 miles (40 km) from Athens. The runner Pheidippides brought news of the victory to Athens, where he died shouting, "Rejoice! We conquer!" Now more than 2,000 years later, the marathon would start at the site of the historic battle.

Seventeen contestants began the race. Runners from France and Australia took the early lead. Then the crowds of people lining the route let out a roar as the Greek shepherd, Spiridon Louis, took command.

Louis finally made it into the stadium, still ahead of the nearest runner. Though exhausted, he made his way along the straightaway toward the finish line as the roaring crowd urged him on.

When Louis crossed the finish line, thousands of spectators began a national celebration. Some hugged and kissed each other, while others cried with joy. Not only had the little shepherd restored national pride, he had given life to the modern Olympic Games.

The Long-Distance Runner

Paavo Nurmi was the greatest long-distance runner of his time. He began his Olympic career at the 1920 Antwerp Games where he won the 10,000 meters and the silver in the 5,000 meters. Four years later in Paris, France, Nurmi performed a feat that still stands as one of the greatest track and field performances in Olympic history.

On July 10, 1924, Nurmi was scheduled to run the 1,500-meter race. One hour later, he would compete in the 5,000 meters. No Olympic athlete had ever made such an attempt.

No one was surprised when Nurmi won the 1,500 meters. But in the 5,000 meters, he would have to face fellow countryman Ville Ritola, who already had won two gold medals.

With 300 meters remaining, Ritola led Nurmi—and showed no signs of slowing down. Nurmi attempted to pass, but Ritola refused to give up the lead. Most runners would have given up at that point. But on the final turn, Nurmi made another attempt— and this time won the race.

Nurmi added three more gold medals to his Olympic total. Four years later in Amsterdam, Nurmi won another gold in the 10,000 meters and two silver in the 5,000 meters and 3,000-meter steeplechase. Though he was 31 years old, Nurmi had established himself as the greatest long-distance runner in Olympic history.

Paavo Nurmi competes in the 5,000 meter race.

The Superior Athlete

One year before the 1936 Berlin Olympics, Jesse Owens set three world records while matching a fourth in a track meet in Ann Arbor, Michigan. His Olympic victories in the 100 meters, long jump, 200 meters, and in the 4 x 100 relay in Berlin made him famous. But Owens almost left the Olympics with only three gold medals.

The German champion Luz Long saved Owens in the long jump. In the qualifying round, Owens had three attempts to make it to the final. But he fouled twice. Owens was afraid that he would fail on his third and last attempt to qualify and not make it to the final. Then Long approached him.

"Jesse," he said, "let me make a suggestion. I will place my towel a foot in front of the foul line and you can use this for your takeoff. You should then qualify easily."

Owens followed Long's advice, and made his qualifying jump. He then went on to defeat the German champion in the same event.

After Owen's victory, Long was the first one to congratulate him. The two walked arm in arm in front of Adolf Hitler's box. Hitler, the leader of Nazi Germany, had hoped the Berlin Olympics would prove to the world that his athletes were superior to any on Earth. Instead, it was Owens who proved to be the superior athlete. Owens never saw Luz Long again. He was killed in World War II.

Owens' record of 4 track and field gold medals in the same Olympics stood for 48 years. Carl Lewis finally matched that feat at the 1984 Los Angeles Olympics in the same 4 events.

Zatopek's Marathon

July 24, 1952, at the Olympic Games in Helsinki was a special day for Emil Zatopek. The great Czechoslovakian distance runner had just won the gold in the 5,000 meters. A few days earlier, he won the gold in the 10,000 meters. With the gold and silver medals he won in the 10,000 meters and 5,000 meters four years earlier in London, Zatopek had three gold medals to show for his Olympic career.

After Zatopek left the ceremony in which he received his medal, he saw the women's javelin-throw contestants entering the field. His wife, Dana, was among them. Proudly he showed her the gold medal, then handed it to her for good luck.

On her first throw, Dana broke the Olympic record. The Zatopeks became the first and only married couple ever to win Olympic medals on the same day in separate events.

Despite the amazing accomplishment, Zatopek was not satisfied. He wanted more. "I think I'll try the marathon," he told one surprised reporter. On the final day of the track and field competition, Zatopek entered the 26-mile (42-m) marathon—a race he had never run before.

Jim Peters of Great Britain was the heavy favorite to win the marathon. Before the race, Zatopek introduced himself to Peters and asked to run with him. Peters agreed.

At the start of the race, the pace was very fast. Zatopek was tiring, but Peters looked as though he could run forever.

Emil Zatopek (left) and his wife display their gold medals after the 1952 Olympics.

"I couldn't believe what was happening," said Zatopek. "So I said to [Peters], 'Isn't the pace too fast?' Jim said in jest, 'No, it's too slow'. . . so I believed him."

Instead of waiting for Peters, Zatopek ran faster—and left him behind. When Zatopek entered the stadium, 80,000 people began cheering his name. Emil Zatopek then won his third gold medal in Helsinki. Peters never finished the race. He collapsed from exhaustion along the route and was taken to the hospital.

Number Three for Papp

Floyd Patterson, Muhammad Ali, Joe Frazier, George Foreman, and Sugar Ray Leonard are some of the most famous fighters who used their Olympic experience to win professional championship titles. Though an Olympic boxing legend, Hungary's Laszlo Papp never had the chance to become a professional boxing champion.

At the 1948 London Games, Papp won the gold medal as a middleweight. Four years later in Helsinki, Papp entered the light-middleweight division. He breezed through the five-bout competition without a defeat—scoring two of his victories by knockouts.

Having already won two gold medals when the 1956 Melbourne Games approached, the 30-year-old Papp decided to go for the gold one more time. Papp had no trouble with the competition. In the light-middleweight final, he faced Jose Torres of the United States, who would eventually become light-heavyweight champion of the world. In a tough, close fight, Papp won on a decision—and received his third gold medal.

With the win, Papp became the first boxer in Olympic history to win three gold medals. One year later, Papp became the first athlete from a Communist country to turn professional.

Papp went undefeated in 30 professional fights. But he never fought for a championship title. When he was 38, he retired and began training young Hungarian boxers for future Olympic Games.

Olympic boxing
legend Laszlo Papp.

The Yale Crew

Since the 1900 Games in Paris, the eight-oar crew race had been dominated by America. Before the start of the 1956 Summer Games, U.S. crews had won 9 of the 11 gold medals.

But in their qualifying race in Melbourne, Australia, the United States team from Yale University finished third behind the Australian and Canadian crews. Only the first two finishers reach the next round.

The Americans had one last chance. They would have to win the repechage, the race that gives a final opportunity for all the teams that failed to qualify. Even if the U.S. won, they had history stacked against them. Never had any team won the gold medal after losing its qualifying race.

The United States faced Italy, Great Britain and France. A victory put the Americans in the semifinal race against Australia, one of the teams that defeated them in the qualifying round. Again, the Americans won the race as Australia came in second.

On November 27, 1956, the United States crew took on Australia, Sweden, and Canada in the 2,000-meter final. America trailed with 500 meters remaining. Then, rowing at 40 strokes per minute, the United States forged ahead.

The U.S. crew crossed the finish line first, followed by Canada, Australia, and Sweden. With the win, the American team from Yale made Olympic history: the first team ever to win a gold medal after losing the qualifying round.

The Yale crew.

The World's Fastest Woman

Perhaps no Olympic champion had greater childhood hardships than Wilma Rudolph. When she was very young, Wilma had to walk with a brace on her left leg until she was 11 years old. Nine years later, she would win three gold medals at the 1960 Rome Olympics—becoming one of America's most beloved athletes.

But Wilma's triumph in Rome did not begin well. The day before her qualifying race in the 100-meter event, she tripped over a water pipe and severely sprained her ankle. But that night, the swelling went down. Wilma would make it to the starting line, but she had to keep her ankle taped throughout the Olympics.

Despite the injury, Rudolph won the gold medal in the 100-meter race. Even more remarkable, she won another in the 200 meters. Then to top off her glorious day, Wilma ran the anchor leg on the victorious 4 x 10 relay team. Rudolph became the star of the 1960 Olympic Games as newspapers all over the world called her "the fastest woman in the world."

Opposite page: Wilma Rudolph (Center), Olympic champion.

Cuthbert Strikes Gold

At the 1956 Melbourne Olympics, no female star shined more than Betty Cuthbert of Australia. Cuthbert entered three events—the 100 meters, 200 meters and 4 x 100 relay. In the 100-meter final, Cuthbert was an underdog against her teammate, Marlene Mathews. But Cuthbert easily won as Mathews finished third. In the 200-meter race, Cuthbert put on a late charge and won by a few feet. A few days later, she anchored the Australian 4 x 100 relay team and won her third gold. Cuthbert was the toast of Australia.

Many experts thought that Cuthbert would also shine at the 1960 Rome Olympics. But a few months before the Games began, Cuthbert pulled a hamstring. Thinking her leg had healed, Cuthbert looked forward to winning more gold medals. But in the second round of the 100 meters, her injury returned, and she was eliminated. Cuthbert also had to withdraw from the 200 meters and 4 x 100 relay. Suddenly, her Olympic career seemed to be over.

Cuthbert retired in 1960. But as the 1964 Olympics in Tokyo approached, she got the urge to run again. Cuthbert entered the 400-meter race, clearly an underdog. She had finished third in her qualifying heat and second in the semifinal. Ann Packer of Great Britain and Australia's Judith Amoore were expected to battle for the gold medal.

The 400 meters was a new event for Cuthbert, who won her previous gold medals as a sprinter. She was fast, but she wondered if she had the strength to endure a long race.

Betty Cuthbert (#468) charges past the finish line to win a gold medal in the women's 100 meters in 1956.

Not surprising, Cuthbert took the early lead. After the first 200 meters, she had a three-meter lead. Cuthbert led the pack all the way into the final stretch. But then Packer made her move, slowly cutting into Cuthbert's lead. It wasn't enough as Cuthbert crossed the finish line two feet ahead. Eight years after winning three gold medals, Betty Cuthbert had won her fourth.

Beamon's Jump

At the 1968 Mexico City Olympics, America's Bob Beamon was on the verge of elimination from the long jump qualification round. His first two attempts were fouls. One more and he would not make the event.

Fellow competitor Ralph Boston approached Beamon and suggested that he take off a foot behind the foul line. Though the resulting jump would probably not be Beamon's best, it would be good enough to qualify. Beamon took Boston's advice—and advanced to the long jump final.

Later in the afternoon, teammate Lee Evans walked onto the field. Suddenly, the crowd let out a roar. Evans looked across the field to the long jump pit and saw officials and athletes running everywhere. Most noticeably, Bob Beamon was jumping up and down.

After a long delay, the public address system finally announced the historic news. "Bob Beamon's leap, 8.90 meters. . . 29 feet 2.5 inches." The crowd was in shock, some doubting the numbers they had just heard. But then it became official. Beamon's jump was a new world record.

The rest of the competitors stared in disbelief at each other. The competition was already over in the first round.

Opposite page:
Bob Beamon sails to a
new world record in
the long jump.

Korbut's Comeback

During the gymnastics competition at the 1972 Munich Olympics, television cameras zoomed in on 17-year-old Olga Korbut of the Soviet Union as she wept bitterly following her botched performance on the uneven bars. Viewers shared in Korbut's despair as she was eliminated from competing for all-around honors as the Summer Games' best female gymnast.

Two days earlier, Korbut had won the hearts of worldwide audiences, ending her great performance with a captivating smile that endeared her to millions. Now the scenes of Korbut weeping were played and replayed on television all over the world. In disaster, she gained more attention and admiration than her teammate Lyudmila Turishcheva, the eventual all-around winner.

The next day, in the individual apparatus events, Korbut made one of the great comebacks in Olympic history. With the uneven parallel bar mishap behind her, the brightly smiling Korbut won two golds and a silver. Women's gymnastics would never be the same. Korbut's performance and charm brought the sport from obscurity to one of the most high-profile and glamorous events of the Summer Games.

Olga Korbut made one of the great comebacks in the history of the Olympics.

The Basketball Showdown

The greatest basketball controversy in the history of the Olympics took place during the gold medal battle between the United States and the Soviet Union at the 1972 Munich Games.

Up to this point in history, the United States had won every gold medal since basketball was added to the Games in 1936. America had gone undefeated in 62 straight games over 8 Olympic competitions.

But at Munich, the U.S struggled against the Soviet Union, and trailed 49-48 with six seconds left in the game. Suddenly, Doug Collins of the U.S. picked up a loose ball at mid-court and drove for the basket. Though he missed the layup, he was fouled with three seconds left in the game.

Collins sunk both free throws for a 50-49 United States lead. The Soviets put the ball in play and reached mid-court when they called a time-out. The referee's whistle stopped the clock with one second left—even though the Soviets had no time-outs remaining. Though the Soviets had called an illegal time-out, they were given another opportunity to put the ball in play.

The Soviets threw the ball in and took a long, desperate shot from mid-court that missed the mark. The buzzer sounded and the United States celebrated an apparent 50-49 win.

But then the Soviets approached the scorer's table and protested that the clock was not set back to the original three seconds. The clock was reset, and the Soviets had another chance.

For a third time, the Soviets put the ball in play. This time, a long, full-court pass was lobbed in the direction of 6-foot 8-inch forward Alexander Belova, who stood beneath the basket. Belov caught the ball between two American defenders and laid it in the basket as the buzzer sounded. The Soviets celebrated a 51-50 win—one of the biggest upsets in Olympic history—while the shocked U.S. team looked on.

The United States petitioned the International Olympic Committee, offering sworn statements by the referee and timekeeper that the Soviets were not entitled to the victory. Four months later, the IOC handed down its final decision. The United States' protest was denied—and the Soviet Union was officially declared the winner of the gold medal.

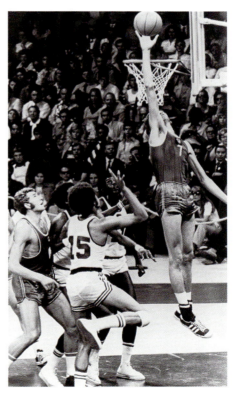

At the medal awards ceremony, the Soviet team stood on the top step of the victory podium. To their left, the team from Cuba prepared to receive their bronze medals. The silver medal level remained empty. The United States team refused to appear. To this day, none of the U.S players have accepted their second-place medals.

A Soviet player blocks a shot in the last minutes of the game.

27

Seven Gold Medals

Mark Spitz made Olympic history at the 1972 Munich Games by winning seven gold medals in swimming. Even more remarkable, each performance set a world record.

In his first event, Spitz won the 200-meter butterfly. A few hours later, Spitz swam the anchor leg in the 4 x 100 meter freestyle relay for his second gold medal.

When the individual times for each American were released, Spitz's teammate, Jerry Heidenreich, had a faster time than Spitz. Some experts predicted that Heidenreich would defeat Spitz in the upcoming 100-meter freestyle.

In the next three days, Spitz took gold medals in the 200-meter freestyle and the 100-meter butterfly. Spitz also swam the anchor leg for the American 4 x 200 relay team for his fifth gold medal and fifth world record.

But Spitz was getting tired. He told his coach, Sherm Chavoor, to pull him from the 100-meter freestyle so he could be fresh for the 4 x 100 medley relay. But Chavoor stated that if Spitz didn't swim the 100 meters, he would be out of the relay. "They'll say you're 'chicken'—that you're afraid to face Jerry Heidenreich," Chavoor said.

Spitz entered the 100 meters—and beat Heidenreich by a few feet. He finished the Olympics by winning his seventh gold medal with the 4 x 100 medley relay team, which also set a world record. Never in the history of the Olympics had there been such a swimming champion.

Swimmer Mark Spitz in the 400-meter medley race.

Perfect Nadia

In the 1976 Montreal Olympics, 13-year-old Nadia Comaneci of Romania became an international gymnastics star. But her incredible Olympic performance began with some confusion.

In the uneven parallel bar competition, Comaneci performed flawlessly. But the crowd grumbled as the number "1" flashed on the scoreboard. It was not programmed to register a "10," which is a perfect score. Finally, it was announced that Comaneci had earned a perfect "10" from the judges.

Romania finished second behind the Soviet Union in the team competition. But Comaneci was the real winner. She received her second and third perfect "10s" in the uneven bars and the balance beam. The following day, she earned five more—including two in the individual balance beam and uneven bar competitions.

When the week was over, Comaneci had been awarded seven perfect scores while winning three golds, one silver, and one bronze medal. Even more, she became the first Romanian in history to win an Olympic gymnastic gold medal.

Opposite page: Nadia Comaneci of Romania skyrocketed to international fame at the young age of 13.

Bittersweet Boycott

Before the opening day ceremonies of the 1976 Montreal Olympics, politics intruded into the Games as Kenya joined the African boycott to protest the appearance of New Zealand's rugby team. Months earlier, New Zealand had played in South Africa—a country that had been barred from the Olympics because of their racial discrimination policies. The African countries also wanted the International Olympic Committee to punish New Zealand. When their request was turned down, they decided to boycott the Games. Only Senegal and Ivory Coast chose to compete.

Kenyan runner Mike Boit was looking forward to one of the greatest 800-meter finals in Olympic history. He would face Alberto Juantorena of Cuba and Rick Wohlhuter of the United States. But because of the boycott, the great Olympic showdown would not materialize. Instead, Boit had to watch the race in silence from the stands.

Juantorena set a world record as he crossed the finish line. With the victory, he became the first person from a non-English speaking country to win the gold in the 800 meters.

Boit was silent as the crowd cheered Juantorena during his victory lap.

"Do you think you could have won?" a writer asked Boit. Tears filled Boit's eyes. "We'll never know, will we?" he said. "We'll never know." Politics had ruined one of the greatest races never run.

Kenya's Mike Boit (right) leads the pack in the pre-Olympic 1,000-meter race in 1976.

The Boxing Legend

Some experts believe that the greatest Olympic heavyweight champion of all time could have been one of the greatest professional fighters ever. But Cuban boxing legend, Teofilo Stevenson, never fought for a world championship title.

At the 1972 Munich Olympic Games, the 20-year-old, 6-foot 3-inch Stevenson took the world by storm with his powerful boxing skills. To get to the final, Stevenson won all his matches by technical knockout. Then he became Olympic champion without throwing a punch. His opponent had to withdraw because of injury.

Four years later in Montreal, Stevenson continued his knockout string all the way to the final. There, he met Romanian fighter Mircea Simon. Simon stayed away from Stevenson's long jabs for more than two rounds. Then Stevenson hit him with a powerful blow that sent Simon reeling. Before long, Simon's manager waved a white towel. Simon could not return to the ring. Stevenson had won his second gold medal.

Financial offers poured in from America. But Stevenson turned them down. "I love my country," he would always say, "and they love me. I want to keep it this way."

At the 1980 Moscow Games, the 28-year-old Stevenson was already an Olympic boxing legend. Opponents were happy just to be standing at the end of their three-round fight with the Cuban. Stevenson won his third and final gold medal by winning a 4 to 1 decision over his Soviet opponent. After the match, he retired. Never had the Olympics seen such a boxing champion.

Teofilo Stevenson, Olympic heavyweight boxing champion.

Edwin Moses

At the 1984 Summer Games in Los Angeles, 28-year-old Edwin Moses of the United States was the big favorite to win the men's 400-meter hurdles race. Eight years earlier at the 1976 Montreal Games, Moses won the gold medal by one of the greatest margins in history, defeating teammate Michael Shine by more than a second. It seemed as though he would go on to become an Olympic legend. But Moses did not compete in the 1980 Moscow Games because of the American boycott.

It did not get any better for Moses. He could not race in 1982 because of injuries. Months before the 1984 Olympics, Moses' father died after a short illness.

Now, moments before the start of the 400-meter hurdles, hundreds of cameras were clicking. Moses and several others jumped the gun, but none were charged with a false start.

Finally, the race began. After 50 meters, Moses sprinted into the lead—and never slowed down. The crowd roared as Moses headed into the final turn, building on his big lead. Once he cleared the last hurdle, the race was his.

Moses took his victory lap. Then he spotted his wife and mother, who had left their seats to join him on the field. Moses hugged them as he started to cry.

"I won this one for Dad, I won this one for Dad," he said.

Opposite page:
Olympic track star
Edwin Moses.

Carl Lewis: The Best Ever

At the 1984 Summer Games in Los Angeles, Carl Lewis joined Jesse Owens in the Olympic record books by winning four gold medals—in the 100- and 200-meter dash, the long jump, and as part of the 4 x 100-meter relay team.

Four years later in Seoul, South Korea, Lewis won two more gold medals with victories in the 100-meter and long jump. He also added a silver in the 200-meter.

At the 1992 Barcelona Olympics, the 31-year-old Lewis won his seventh gold medal with his third consecutive long jump victory. His eighth gold medal came as he anchored the 4 x 100 relay team.

And then, at the age of 35, in the 1996 Atlanta Olympics, against all odds, Lewis won his ninth gold medal with his fourth Olympic long jump victory. He barely qualified for the long jump competition, making it on his last attempt in the qualifying round. The next night, Lewis nailed a jump of 27 feet, 10 3/4 inches (8.5 meters), easily leaving his competition in the dust.

Carl Lewis arrived at the Olympics in 1984 a champion and left the Olympics in 1996 a champion. In four Olympic Games, Carl Lewis became, simply, the best ever track and field star in Olympic history.

Opposite page:
Carl Lewis' golden Olympic moments (clockwise from top left): long jump (1984), 4x100 meter relay (1984), long jump (1996), long jump (1992). Center: celebrating his ninth gold medal (1996).

Retton's Perfect "10"

On August 3, 1984, at the Summer Games in Los Angeles, 36 finalists for the individual all-around women's gymnastic title prepared for their four events: uneven bars, balance beam, vault, and floor exercise.

The favorite to win the gold was Ecaterina Szabo of Romania. Sixteen-year-old Mary Lou Retton of the United States wasn't given much of a chance. At four feet, nine inches tall and weighing 92 pounds, Retton had never competed in a major international event before the Los Angeles Games. Still, Retton was in first place, 15 hundredths of a point in front of Szabo before the individual all-around competition began.

Szabo scored a perfect 10 on the balance beam. Retton performed well on the uneven parallel bars, but did not retain her first-place lead. After the first round, the two gymnasts were tied. On the balance beam, Szabo scored a 9.95 while Retton was awarded a 9.80. Szabo now led by 15 hundredths of a point.

Szabo was awarded 9.90 on the vault.   But Retton scored a perfect 10 in the floor exercise. With one event remaining, Retton trailed the Romanian by only five hundredths of a point.

Szabo finished the night with a 9.90 on the uneven bars. Retton needed a perfect score on the vault to win the gold medal.

The stadium was silent as Retton eyed the vault, then began her run. She landed on the horse firmly with both hands, twirled through the air, then performed a flawless landing. The crowd roared its approval.

***Mary Lou Retton triumphed
at the 1984 Olympics.***

After a short delay, Retton's score was flashed throughout
the stadium. She had scored a perfect "10." With the win, Retton
became the first American gymnast to ever win the overall title.

The Heptathlon

On September 23, 1988, at the Summer Games in Seoul, South Korea, 29 women prepared for the start of the seven-event heptathlon that would determine the finest all-around woman athlete in the world.

Jackie Joyner-Kersee of the United States was the favorite. She had dominated the event in the two years of international competition leading to the Seoul Games, winning it nine straight times. Even more impressive, Joyner-Kersee had scored more than 7,000 points on four different occasions—a mark no other woman had ever reached.

In the 100-meter hurdles, Joyner-Kersee sprinted into the lead and finished four points better than her own world record pace set at the Olympic trials.

In the high jump, Joyner-Kersee strained her left knee. Still, she retained her overall lead—but was 87 points off her world record. With her leg taped, Joyner-Kersee got off her second longest throw in the shotput. Then she finished the day with a victory in the 200-meter dash. But she was more than 100 points off her world mark.

The next day, Joyner-Kersee competed in the long jump and easily beat the competition. Now she was within 11 points of her world record. Joyner-Kersee did not perform well in the javelin and lost many points. But she still kept her overall lead.

In the two-lap race, Jackie was in fifth place after one lap. But she stayed within striking distance of the leaders and didn't feel tired. When she crossed the finish line, Joyner-Kersee had run

**Olympic track star
Jackie Joyner-Kersee.**

her second fastest 800 meters ever. With the victory, she broke her own world record by 76 points.

Four days following her heptathlon triumph, Joyner-Kersee broke the Olympic record in the women's long jump, winning her second gold medal in Seoul. Her overall performance was one of the greatest in Olympic history.

The Dive of Death

Diver Greg Louganis became a star at the 1984 Los Angeles Games. He won the springboard event by the largest margin in Olympic history. Then on his final dive in the platform event, Louganis prepared to become the first diver in Olympic history to score more than 700 points.

His final dive was a reverse 3.5 somersault. Because the dive is so difficult, it is known as "the Dive of Death." Louganis leaped off the tower, then emerged from the pool to thunderous applause. His final score was 710—a new Olympic record.

Four years later in Seoul, South Korea, Louganis went for victories in the springboard and diving events. But in the springboard eliminations, Louganis struck his head on the board. Fortunately, he was not seriously injured, and went on to qualify.

With one dive remaining, Xiong Ni of China led Louganis by three points. Ni's last dive was nearly perfect. Louganis decided to perform "the Dive of Death." He had to be perfect.

Louganis walked to the platform edge and made a flawless dive. The crowd roared with delight. Greg Louganis had become only one of two divers ever to win the springboard and diving events.

Opposite page: Olympic diving champion Greg Louganis.

The Dream Team

When it came to Olympic basketball, every competing country always put its best team forward for the Games—every country, that is, except for the United States. Because "professional" basketball players were not allowed to compete, the U.S. always assembled a team of the best college players in the country. With these college All-Stars, America had won every gold medal in basketball since it entered Olympic competition in 1936. But then came the upset in 1972. Since that time, the U.S. pushed for a rule change that would allow NBA players to compete in the Olympics. Their efforts grew after the U.S. settled for the bronze medal in 1988.

In April 1989, FIBA, the international basketball federation, adopted the rule change. And so, the "Dream Team" was born: Magic Johnson, Larry Bird, Michael Jordan, Patrick Ewing, Chris Mullin, John Stockton, Karl Malone, Scottie Pippen, Charles Barkley, Clyde Drexler, and David Robinson—each one an All-Star. Christian Laettner, the best player in college ball that year, was also added to the team.

Never had a team been assembled for international competition that was this good. The rest of the world knew that the gold medal in basketball was not available. The highlight for most opponents was just to be on the same court with the Dream Team. Most made sure they had their pictures taken with the U.S. squad once the rout was over.

Dream Team members (from left to right): Michael Jordan, Patrick Ewing, and Scottie Pippen.

The toughest job for U.S. Coach Chuck Daly was finding enough time to play all his All-Stars. He did a great job juggling huge egos, and the Dream Team was a great success, averaging 127.3 points a game and winning by an average of 43.8. The Dream Team never scored less than 100 points, and never allowed an opponent near 90. The closest outcome was a 32-point victory over Croatia in the gold-medal game.

There may never be a better team.

Redmond's Glory

On August 3, 1992, eight men prepared for the first semifinal 400 meters at the Barcelona Olympics. The favorite was defending Olympic champion Steve Lewis of the United States.

Derek Redmond of Great Britain was expected to challenge him. Redmond easily won his preliminary races, and looked forward to winning a medal.

But throughout his career, Redmond had been plagued by injuries. At the 1988 Seoul Games, Redmond was favored to win a medal, but never ran a race. He had to withdraw because of a pulled Achilles tendon. Later, other injuries forced him to miss the European championships and the Commonwealth Games. He was feeling good heading into the Barcelona Games.

At the start of the 400-meter race, Redmond got off quickly. Then he sprinted down the backstretch toward the halfway point. Getting ready to make his turn around the bend, Redmond suddenly heard a funny pop. The hamstring in his right leg was torn.

Redmond stood in pain as he watched the other seven runners finish the race. Suddenly, a man stepped to the track and rushed to the injured runner. It was his father, Jim Redmond.

"Look, you don't have to do this," his father said.

"Yes, I do," Redmond replied.

"Well," said his father, "if you're going to finish this race, we'll finish it together."

One of the most memorable scenes in Olympic history suddenly unfolded as Redmond was helped by his father around the track to the finish line. In defeat, Derek Redmond had gained more glory than if he had won a gold medal.

Derek Redmond (left) cries out in pain as he is assisted by his father.

One More Time

Janet Evans' gold medal victory in the 800-meter freestyle at the 1992 Barcelona Summer Games was more rewarding than the three gold medals she won in the 1988 Seoul Summer Olympics.

"Those came a lot easier," she said after becoming the first woman to win back-to-back 800s in the Olympics. "I honestly don't know if it's my last race. I know I'm going to take a long, long break."

The 21-year-old Evans beat Australia's Hayley Jane Lewis by nearly five seconds, breaking out early and coasting to the win. Being part of a young and improved U.S. team took some pressure off her. But in Seoul, nobody expected anything because she was just "a little girl" going up against the powerful East Germans.

Evans admitted it would be difficult to do something with her life that would compare with the victory lap she took around the Olympic pool.

"It's great to see the American flags waving and have people pulling for you from various countries," she said. "I needed to do this for myself. I had to do it one more time."

Evans' Olympic saga did not end there. In the 1996 Atlanta Summer Games, Evans came up short in her bid to win a fifth gold medal. But she still had five Olympic medals, three world records, and 45 national titles to her credit. Most of all, she came away as a true champion. "Winning gold medals is fun," she said. "But I've learned a lot this time about what the Olympics are all about. It's about getting out there and doing your best—and being happy with yourself for trying."

Michael Makes History

The world said there was no male runner who could win gold medals in both the 200- and 400-meter races. Track experts said these races demanded skills too different to expect one athlete to compete in both at a world-class level. Michael Johnson of the United States didn't listen to the experts. Instead, he won both races in record-setting fashion.

In the 400-meter race, Johnson set an Olympic record with a time of 43.49 seconds to earn his first-ever gold medal. It took Michael many years to accomplish his goal of getting a medal. At times, he thought of giving up. In 1988, he missed a chance at the Seoul Olympics because of a broken leg. In 1992, he came down with food poisoning at the Barcelona Olympics. But at the 1996 Atlanta Games, he not only had his first medal, he had a chance at making history.

Just three days after winning the 400-meter, Johnson, wearing a gold chain around his neck, a gold earring in his left ear, and gold running shoes, took to the starting blocks to see if he could be the first man in history to win both events.

In lane three, Johnson, the son of a truck driver and grade school teacher, readied for the greatest race of his life.

The gun went off and the runners raced out of the blocks. Michael stumbled briefly in the beginning only to turn it up and blast past the rest of the field. "I was running pretty fast," said Johnson. "I just relaxed. I couldn't go any faster."

The thousands of flashbulbs from the cameras in the stadium's seats looked like fireflies in the night.

Michael Johnson sprints toward a world record in the 200-meter race.

With five meters to go, Michael felt a twinge in his right hamstring. But he burst through the pain and crossed the finish line, three full strides ahead of the nearest competitor. Johnson extended his arms as the home-crowd cheered wildly and then gasped, noticing the scoreboard's "19:32"—a new world record!

The world said that no male could win the 200- and 400-meter races in the same Olympics. And for many years no one did. But then Michael Johnson proved everyone wrong by making history.

"Ever since I started, my career was based on the 200 and the 400—and bringing those two events together like no person had ever done," Johnson said.

Michael did bring the two events together, in Olympic and world record fashion—like no other person had done before.

The Golden Girls

A few months before the 1996 Summer Games in Atlanta, Kerri Strug's coaches wondered if she had what it takes to be an Olympic gymnastics champion. That concern would be put to the test in Strug's very first vault attempt. A successful routine from her would clinch America's first-ever team gold in Olympic women's gymnastics.

The United States went into the final vault event with a comfortable lead. But then Dominique Moceanu landed on her backside on both her vault tries. Her best score was a 9.2.

Because each team's lowest score per event is tossed out, anything more than 9.2 from Strug would clinch the gold. Strug made her approach, planted her hands firmly on the vault—then landed with a thud that tore ligaments in her left ankle; she also landed on her backside. The judges gave her a 9.162. Now the gold medal was in doubt. How could Strug possibly improve her routine while landing on a bad ankle?

In obvious pain, Strug still made her second try. Drawing upon all the inner strength she could muster, Strug flew down the runway, over the vault, onto the mat—and into Olympic history. Despite her ankle problem, Strug somehow managed to keep both feet on the mat long enough to successfully finish her routine and secure the title. At the same time, she created an image that would go down in Olympic lore. Her heroic performance gave the U.S. Women's Gymnastics Team their first-ever Olympic gold medal.

"I didn't know what was wrong with my foot," Strug said. "But everyone else had put so much time and sacrifice into it. I couldn't give up."

The 4-foot 9-inch, 80-pound Strug didn't always feel that way. Once a member of the 1992 Olympic team, Strug bounced between gyms for four years before coach Bela Karolyi finally gave her another chance. Still, he was concerned about her will to win. She impressed him by taking the American Cup in March—her first international title. But the competition wasn't the best in the world, and Strug still had to prove herself. Her second vault in the Atlanta Games would be her shining moment.

Strug's amazing effort ended the Russians' brief hopes of capturing the gold. They finished second for the first time since 1948. Romania took the bronze medal.

Kerri Strug clinched the gold for the U.S. team with her heroic vault.

After Karolyi carried Strug back into the arena for the awards ceremony, Moceanu and Shannon Miller helped her up two steps on the platform. "We didn't want to march out without Kerri," said team captain Amanda Borden. "She gave it everything she had."

Though Strug's final vault sealed the win, the American team would not have been in the position to earn the gold medal without a total team effort.

Jaycie Phelps and Amanda Borden provided leadership and overall consistency throughout the team events.

Using her tiny, four-foot six-inch, 72-pound frame, Dominique Moceanu mastered the balance beam. And on the floor exercise she brought the capacity crowd to its feet as she performed magnificently.

Amy Chow, who received a silver medal in the individual uneven bars exercise, performed even better for the team.

Dominique Dawes, with a bronze medal in the floor exercise, became the first black woman to win an individual Olympic medal. She performed brilliantly on each event for the team.

And then there was the 19-year-old Shannon Miller who entered the Atlanta Games with nine world championship medals and five Olympic medals to her credit—tops on the U.S. team.

At the 1996 Summer Games, Miller performed almost flawlessly. Besides the team gold, she finished her Olympic career with an individual gold on the balance beam. Her team floor exercise and vault routines gave the U.S. squad the boost it needed to go for the gold.

Miller tried not to think about winning a team Olympic gold medal for the first time in the history of U.S. women's gymnastics. "But maybe a couple of times it went through my head," she admitted.

And when the time came to receive her team gold medal, she couldn't fight back the tears. "It's really hard not to cry when the national anthem is playing and you realize what you've done," she said. "It's such a great feeling of pride for your country."

The U.S. women's gymnastics team celebrates its gold medal victory.

More Unforgettable Moments

1900—Charles Bennett sets the world record in the 1,500-meter race.

1912—Jim Thorpe wins the decathlon and the title of the world's greatest athlete.

1912—Hannes Kolehmainen sets the world record in the 5,000-meter race.

1920—Joseph Guillemot defeats Paavo Nurmi in the 5,000-meter run.

1924—Vilho Ritola sets the world record in the 10,000-meter race.

1928—Betty Robinson becomes the first female track gold medal winner in Olympic history.

1928—Paavo Yrjola wins the men's decathlon.

1932—William Carr sets the world record in the 400-meter race.

1932—Thomas Hampson sets the world record in the 800-meter race.

1936—Jack Lovelock sets the world record in the 1,500-meter race.

1948—Sammy Lee wins the gold medal in diving.

1952—Harrison Dillard wins four gold medals in track and field.

1952—Emil Zatopek wins his fourth gold medal in men's long distance running.

1952—Lindy Remigino wins two gold medals in track and field.

1956—The Hungarian water polo team goes undefeated and wins the gold medal.

1956—Norman Read wins the gold medal in the 50 kilometer walking race.

1956—Pat McCormick wins her fourth gold medal in women's diving.

1956—Agness Keleti wins four gold medals in women's gymnastics.

1960—Abebe Bikila wins the men's marathon.

1960—The U.S. men's relay swim team sets two world records and wins two gold medals.

1960—Cassius Clay (Muhammad Ali) wins the gold in heavyweight boxing.

1960—Rafer Johnson wins the men's decathlon.

1960—Otis Davis sets the world record in the 400-meter race.

1960—Herb Elliott sets the world record in the 1,500-meter race.

1960—John Devitt defeats Lance Larson in the men's 100-meter freestyle event.

Cassius Clay (right) wins on decision.

1964—Billy Mills becomes the first American to win the 10,000-meter race.

1964—The Japanese women's volleyball team wins the gold medal.

1964—Dawn Fraser wins her third consecutive gold medal in the 100-meter freestyle.

1964—Joe Frazier wins the gold in heavyweight boxing.

1964—Peter Snell wins his second consecutive gold medal in the 800-meter run.

1964—Betty Cuthbert wins her fourth gold medal in women's track and field.

1968—Vera Caslavska wins four gold and two silver medals in gymnastics.

1968—Tommie Smith sets the world record in the 200-meter race.

1968—Al Oerter wins his fourth consecutive gold medal in the discus throw.

1968—Kip Keino defeats Jim Ryun in the men's 1,500 meter run.

1968—Lee Evans sets the world record in the 400-meter race.

1968—Jim Hines sets the world record in the 100-meter race.

1972—Lasse Viren wins the gold in the 10,000-meter race.

1976—The Japanese men's gymnastic team wins its fifth-consecutive gold medal.

1976—Viktor Saneyev wins his third consecutive gold medal in the triple jump.

1976—Alberto Juantorena sets a world record in the men's 800-meter race.

1980—Vladimir Salnikov wins three gold medals in men's swimming.

1980—Sugar Ray Leonard wins a gold medal in boxing.

1980—Kornelia Ender wins a record-four gold medals in women's swimming.

Sugar Ray Leonard throws a jab.

1980—John Naber wins four gold medals in men's swimming.

1980—Bruce Jenner wins the men's decathlon.

1984—Sebastian Coe wins his second consecutive gold in the 1,500-meter race.

1984—Michael Gross sets a world record in the 200-meter freestyle.

1984—The U.S. men's gymnastic team wins its first gold medal in 80 years.

1984—Ulrike Meyfarth wins the gold medal in the women's high jump and becomes only the second athlete in Olympic history to win a gold medal 12 years apart in the same event.

1984—Daley Thompson wins his second straight decathlon gold medal.

Bruce Jenner celebrates his decathlon victory.

1984—Yasuhiro Yamashita wins the gold medal in judo.

1984—Joan Benoit wins the first women's marathon gold medal.

1984—Carlos Lopez sets the Olympic record in the men's marathon.

1984—Joaquim Cruz sets the Olympic record in the 800-meter race.

1984—Jeff Blatnick wins the gold for the U.S. in super heavyweight Greco-Roman wrestling.

1984—Said Aouita sets the Olympic record in the 5,000-meter race.

1988—Greg Barton becomes the first American to win a kayak gold medal and the first kayaker to win two gold medals in 90 minutes.

1988—Kristin Otto wins six gold medals in women's swimming.

1988—Matt Biondi wins seven medals—including five gold—in men's swimming.

1988—The U.S. 4 x 100 meter medley team (men's swimming) sets a new world record.

1988—Florence Griffith Joyner sets the record for women's 100-meter and 200-meter races.

1988—Guennadi Avdeenko sets the Olympic record in the high jump.

1988—Sergey Bubka sets the Olympic record for the pole vault.

1988—Ulf Timmermann sets the Olympic record for the shot put.

1988—Carl Lewis sets the world record in the men's 100-meter race.

Florence Griffith Joyner wins the 100-meter race in 1988.

1988—Jurgen Schult sets the Olympic record for the discus throw.

1988—Brahim Boutaib sets the Olympic record in the 10,000-meter race.

1992—Alexander Popov sets the men's 50-meter freestyle Olympic record.

1992—Jan Zelezny sets the Olympic record for men's javelin throw.

1992—Evelyn Ashford leads the U.S. women's 4 x 100 meter relay team to the gold medal.

1992—Quincy Watts sets the Olympic record in the 400-meter race.

1992—Kevin Young sets the world record in the 400-meter hurdles.

1992—Gail Devers wins the gold medal in the women's 100 hurdles.

1994—Pablo Morales wins two gold medals in men's swimming.

Index